My Emotions
Emosyon Mwen Yo

ANGRY
FACHE

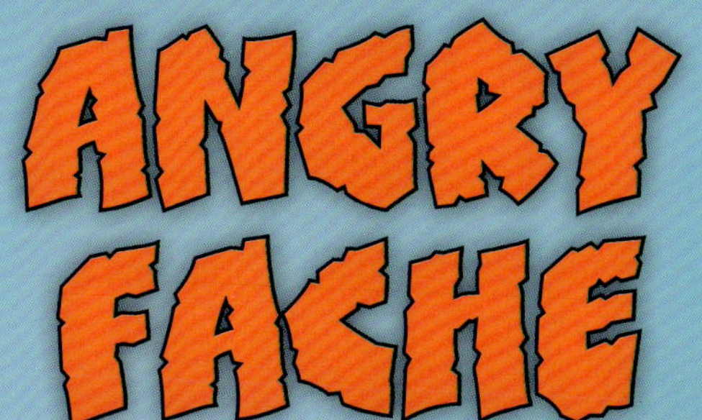

A Crabtree Roots Book
Yon Liv Crabtree Rasin

AMY CULLIFORD
JEAN-PIERRE GASTON

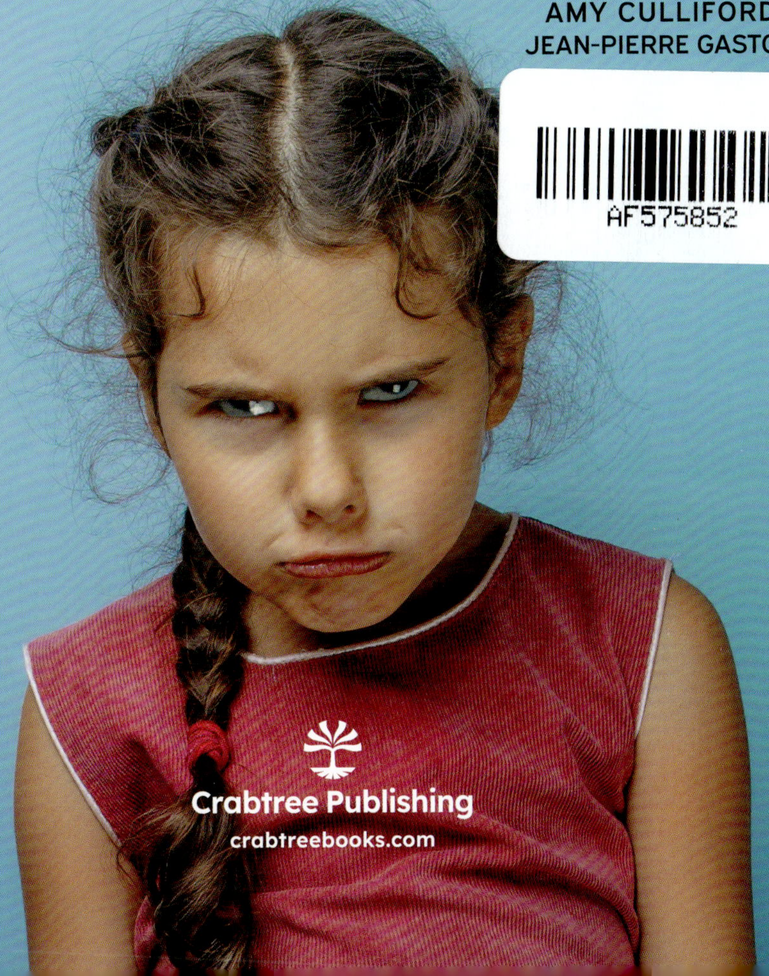

Crabtree Publishing
crabtreebooks.com

School-to-Home Support for Caregivers and Teachers

This book helps children grow by letting them practice reading. Here are a few guiding questions to help the reader with building his or her comprehension skills. Possible answers appear here in red.

Before Reading:

- What do I think this book is about?
    - *This book is about feeling angry.*
    - *This book is about what feeling angry looks or feels like.*

- What do I want to learn about this topic?
    - *I want to learn what to do if I feel angry.*
    - *I want to learn what feeling angry looks like.*

During Reading:

- I wonder why...
    - *I wonder why we yell when we are angry.*
    - *I wonder why we frown when we are angry.*

- What have I learned so far?
    - *I have learned that angry is an emotion.*
    - *I have learned drawing can help when you are angry.*

After Reading:

- What details did I learn about this topic?
    - *I have learned that it is okay to be angry.*
    - *I have learned that there are many ways you can cool down after being angry.*

- Read the book again and look for the vocabulary words.
    - *I see the word* ***vegetables*** *on page 4 and the word* ***yell*** *on page 7. The other vocabulary words are found on page 14.*

What makes me **angry**?

Kisa ki fè mwen **fache**?

I am angry when I eat **vegetables**.

Mwen fache lè mwen ap manje **legim**.

I **yell** when I am angry.

Mwen **rele** lè mwen fache.

I am angry when no one can play.

Mwen fache lè pesonn pa ka vin jwe.

I **frown** when I am angry.

Mwen **fronce sousi** lè mwen fache.

What can I do when I am angry?

Kisa mwen ka fè lè mwen fache?

I can **draw** a picture.

Mwen ka **desine** yon foto.

I can go ride my **bike**.

Mwen ka ale monte **bisiklèt** mwen an.

Words to Know
Mo pouw Konnen

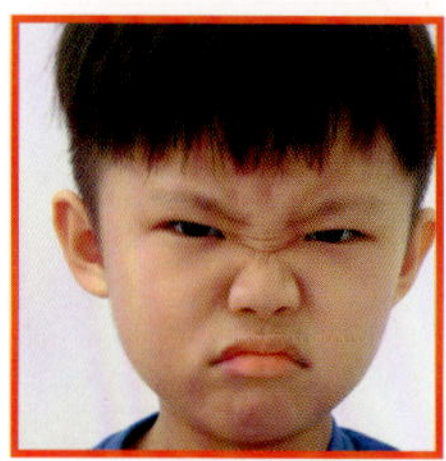

angry
fache

bike
bisiklèt

draw
desine

frown
fronce
sousi

vegetables
legim

yell
rele

50 Words

What makes me **angry**?

I am angry when I eat **vegetables**.

I **yell** when I am angry.

I am angry when no one can play.

I **frown** when I am angry.

What can I do when I am angry?

I can **draw** a picture.

I can go ride my **bike**.

50 mo

Kisa ki fè mwen **fache**?

Mwen fache lè mwen ap manje **legim**.

Mwen **rele** lè mwen fache.

Mwen fache lè pesonn pa ka vin jwe.

Mwen **fronce sousi** lè mwen fache.

Kisa mwen ka fè lè mwen fache?

Mwen ka **desine** yon foto.

Mwen ka ale monte **bisiklèt** mwen an.

My Emotions

ANGRY

Emosyon Mwen Yo

FACHE

Written by: Amy Culliford

Designed by: Rhea Wallace

Series Development: James Earley

Proofreader: Ellen Rodger

Educational Consultant: Marie Lemke M.Ed.

Photographs:

Shutterstock: Juan Pablo Gonzaález: cover; maxim ibragimov: p. 1; TY Lim: p. 3, 14; thevisualsyou need: p. 5, 14; wavebreakmedia: p. 6, 14; Olga Enger: p. 8-9, 14; Mandy Godbehear: p. 10; Julia Kuzhetsova: p. 11, 14; Spotmatik Ltd: p. 13, 14

Crabtree Publishing

crabtreebooks.com 800-387-7650

Printed in Printed in China/082022/FE052422CT

Published in Canada
Crabtree Publishing
616 Welland Ave.
St. Catharines, Ontario
L2M 5V6

Published in the United States
Crabtree Publishing
347 Fifth Avenue,
Suite 1402-145
New York, NY, 10016

Library and Archives Canada Cataloguing in Publication
Available at the Library and Archives Canada

Library of Congress Cataloging-in-Publication Data
Available at the Library of Congress

Paperback: 9781039624559
Ebook: 9781039625396
Epub: 9781039624979